CW00950009

THE WIT AND WISDOM OF THE

TALMUD

RABBI DR. REUVEN P. BULKA

ILLUSTRATIONS BY
JEFF HILL

PETER PAUPER PRESS, INC.
White Plains • New York

INTRODUCTION

☞ *What is the Talmud? — Many religions of the world have based themselves, in one way or another, on the Bible. How they view the Bible determines, to a large extent, the respective differences between these religions. Judaism views the Bible as the Written Law which is fully expounded and elucidated by the Talmud. The Talmud, as interpretation of the Bible, is that which gives Judaism its form and character.*

☞ *What is the Talmud? — The Talmud is Judaism's link between past and future. As a commentary on the Bible, the basic text of Judaism, it serves as the interpretation of Judaism's historic and religious past. As a development of the Bible, it serves as Judaism's guide and interpretation for the present and future. Looking back, the Talmud is now itself a basic text which has given birth to an endless profusion of commentary and responsa dealing with almost every detail of life.*

3

☞ *What is the Talmud?* — *The Talmud is a conglomerate of dialogue and dialectic, comments and observations discussed and presented in the academies of Jewish learning. The minutes of these learning experiences, transmitted from generation to generation, were codified approximately 1,500 years ago. Originally, the Talmud was an "Oral Law," a verbal and vibrant commentary of the "Written Law," the Bible. The codification of the Talmud was dictated, albeit reluctantly, by the sobering reality that much would be forgotten and lost if it were not recorded.*

☞ *What is the Talmud?* — *More than just a development of laws. In the Talmud, one can find discussions or statements relating to anatomy, astrology, biology, botany, counseling, economics, ethics, education, moral law, politics, psychology, sociology, zoology, etc. Most, if not all of these observations in various fields can easily be applied to the contemporary scene. The Talmud, indeed Judaism, reflects a concern not with the par-*

4

ochialism implied in the term "religion,"
rather a concern with life in its all-em-
bracing totality. "Torah", a term used on
numerous occasions in the present volume, refers to the statements, affirma-
tions, and opinions emanating from the
Bible, Talmud, and other spheres of Jewish literature reflecting on all areas of life.

☞ This small volume is an attempt to
give you, the reader, a sampling of the wit,
wisdom, and broad concerns of the Talmud. Hopefully it will whet your appetite,
but not saturate it.

R. P. B.

THE WIT AND WISDOM
OF THE TALMUD

THE WIT AND WISDOM OF THE

☞ He who has acquired knowledge, what does he lack? He who lacks knowledge, what does he possess?

☞ What is hateful to you, do not unto your neighbor.

☞ More people die from overeating than are victims of starvation.

☞ Until the age of forty, food is more beneficial; after forty, drink is more beneficial.

☞ One should first acquire knowledge and then strive to understand it.

☞ Who is wealthy? — He who has a wife of outstanding virtue.

☞ One should never distinguish one child amongst his children.

☞ It is natural for a benevolent person to seek out the poor.

☞ In my home town, my name carries me; away from home, my clothing.

☞ A beast has no dominion over man until man appears to him as an animal.

☞ Water is cheap, wine expensive; the world can exist without wine, but the world cannot be sustained without water.

Salt is cheap, pepper and spices expensive; the world can exist without pepper and spices, but the world cannot be sustained without salt.

☞ A man should not entreat his friend to dine with him when he knows the friend will refuse. And he should not offer him gifts when he knows the friend will not accept them.

☞ God despises him who has evidence to support his neighbor and withholds it. God despises him who speaks with his mouth unlike what he feels in his heart.

☞ Three things God saw fit to create which, had He not, would have been dictated by logic anyway; that a corpse should become offensive, that the deceased should eventually be forgotten from the heart, and that produce should rot.

☞ Any dwelling which is not built to function in the summer and winter is not a true house.

☞ If man uses the Torah properly it is a medicine of life; if improperly, it can be a deadly poison.

11

☞ If old people tell you to tear down and youngsters tell you to build, tear down and do not build, for the tearing down of older people is construction and the building up of youngsters is destruction.

☞ Man in his passion lusts only for that which is forbidden to him.

☞ When man sows, it is a matter of doubt whether he will eat; but when man reaps, he will surely eat.

☞ Do not worry about tomorrow's troubles for you know not what tomorrow will bring. Tomorrow may come and you will not be, and it thus turns out you have worried about a world which is not yours.

☞ According to the camel is the load.

☞ He who prays should direct the eyes downward and the heart upward.

☞ It is a moral imperative that orphans pay the debts of their fathers.

☞ If you desire to learn, do not say of that which you do not comprehend, "I understand it." And if you are asked even concerning a trivial matter of which you are uninformed, do not be afraid to say "I do not know." If you are taught but have not grasped the teaching, do not be in fear of saying, "Teach me again." Do not try to convince yourself you really understand.

☞ One should not threaten a child with future punishment. Rather he should either punish the child immediately or control himself and say nothing.

☞ If you are charitable, you merit wealth. If you have been blessed with wealth, perform charity with it.

☞ Be humble and likeable to all people, and specially to the members of your household.

☞ If you desire to gain your fellow's love, involve yourself with his welfare.

☞ It is difficult to assume power. Hard as it is to assume power, it is even more difficult to give it up.

☞ He who honors a friend for the sake of gain will ultimately leave him in disgrace.

☞ Give charity of your own accord and the act will be attributed to you. Do not wait for others to force you, for the act will then be attributed to them.

☞ Do not crave for the table of kings, for your table is greater than theirs and your crown greater than their crown.

☞ Any love which depends on a cause, once the cause disappears, the love disintegrates; but a love independent of any cause will never disintegrate.

☞ He who is easily provoked and easily pacified, his fault is canceled by his virtue. He who is hard to provoke and hard to pacify, his virtue is canceled by his fault.

☞ It is as difficult to acquire Torah knowledge as to acquire gold utensils, and as easy to lose as the breaking of a glass.

☞ If I am not for myself, who will be for me? If I am for myself, what am I? And if not now, when?

☞ Lower yourself and you will be exalted; exalt yourself and you will be lowered.

☞ He who learns quickly and forgets quickly, his advantage is canceled by his disadvantage. He who is slow to learn and slow to forget, his disadvantage is canceled by his advantage.

☞ According to the effort is the reward.

☞ Be a tail for lions rather than a head for foxes.

☞ Teaching a child is like applying ink to a clean paper. Teaching an aged person is like applying ink to a blotted paper.

☞ He whose deeds exceed his wisdom, his wisdom will endure; but he whose wisdom exceeds his deeds, his wisdom will not endure.

☞ If there is no knowledge, there is no understanding; if there is no understanding, there is no knowledge.

☞ It is not within our ability to explain the contentedness of the wicked, and even not the suffering of the righteous.

☞ A bashful person cannot learn; an impatient person cannot teach.

☞ Learning from children is like eating unripe grapes and drinking wine from the press. Learning from older people is like eating ripened grapes and drinking aged wine.

☞ Peace is to the world as yeast is to dough.

☞ Do not look at the vessel, rather at what it contains.

17

☞ There are seven characteristics of a boor and seven of a wise man: The wise man does not speak before him who is greater than himself in wisdom and experience; he does not interrupt the speech of his fellow; he does not answer hastily; he asks questions relevant to the situation and answers to the point; he responds to first things first and last things last; concerning that which he has not learned he says "I have not learned this"; and he concedes to the truth. The reverse of these characteristics is found in the boor.

☞ Who is wise? — He who learns from all men.

Who is strong? — He who controls his inclinations.

Who is wealthy? — He who is content in his portion.

Who is honored? — He who honors others.

☞ Though the wine may belong to the owner, acknowledgment is given to the one who pours it.

☞ Usurers are compared to shedders of blood. Just as he who has shed blood cannot make restitution, so cannot he who exacts usury make restitution.

☞ The glory of God is mankind.

☞ Once a destructive force is allowed to rampage, it does not distinguish between the righteous and the corrupt.

☞ If anyone is left a large inheritance and wishes to lose it, he should wear expensive clothes, use crystal, and hire workers and leave them alone.

☞ If it boils down to sustaining either the poor of your town or the poor of another town, the poor of your town have priority.

☞ If there is only one stone in a pitcher, shaking it will make a loud noise.

☞ If there is anything reproachable in you, be the first to acknowledge it.

☞ What does a good guest say? — See how much the host has extended himself on my behalf! All the trouble he has gone to was on my behalf. — But what does a bad guest say? — What bother has my host really experienced? All that he has done was for the sake of his wife and children.

☞ Be careful to respect an elderly person who has forgotten his knowledge through circumstances beyond his control.

☞ Do not attempt placating someone when his anger is at a peak, nor should you attempt comforting him when his deceased is before him.

☞ To cry over the past is a vain prayer.

☞ He who sees an unfaithful wife in her indignity should resolve to abstain from wine.

☞ A man's wife is like his own person.

☞ Had the Torah not been given, we would have derived modesty from the cat, integrity from the ant, chastity from the dove, and good manners from the rooster.

☞ The trials of gaining an adequate livelihood are twice as difficult as childbirth.

☞ Anyone in whose house the spilling of wine does not cause the same reaction as the spilling of water is not in the category of blessedness.

☞ An heir is the extension of his father.

☞ If one has eaten garlic and his mouth emits a bad odor, shall he eat more garlic so that his breath will be even more offensive?

☞ Through three things man's character may be judged; by his cup, his purse, and his temper. Some say, even by his laughter.

☞ Night was created only for sleep.

☞ In three ways are acts of lovingkindness superior to charity; charity is performed with one's money, lovingkindness with one's money and one's being; charity is for the poor, lovingkindness for the poor and the rich; charity is for the living, lovingkindness for the living and the dead.

☞ When is a child not dependent on its mother? — if, upon awakening from his sleep he does not call out "Mother, Mother."

☞ Who is the true penitent? — He who is twice confronted by the cause of his original offense and is not affected.

☞ Happy is our youth when it has not disgraced our old-age; happy is our old-age when it has atoned for our youth.

☞ He who is arrogant is considered defective.

☞ The Divine Spirit does not reside in any except the joyful heart.

23

☞ We cannot compare him who has gone over his studies 100 times to him who has gone over his studies 101 times.

☞ Much have I learned from my teachers, and from my colleagues more than from my teachers, but from my students more than all.

☞ A righteous man who dies is lost only to his era. It is like one who has lost a pearl. Wherever it is, it is still a pearl, and is lost only to its owner.

☞ In a time when the community is in anguish, one should not say, "I will go home, eat and drink, and rest content." Rather man should always share in the community's anguish.

☞ Man should always be flexible as the reed and never stubborn as the cedar.

☞ Longevity, posterity, and prosperity are less matters of merit and more matters of destiny.

☞ In the days preceding the Messiah, arrogance will abound and dignity will diminish. The vine will yield its fruit yet wine will be expensive. All sin-fearing people will be despised and truth will be concealed. Youngsters will shame their elders; elders will stand up for youngsters. Sons will denigrate their fathers, daughters will rebel against their mothers, and daughters-in-law against their mothers-in-law. Man's enemies will be the members of his own household.

☞ He who has bread in his basket and says, "What will I eat tomorrow?" is of small faith.

☞ Every little penny eventually adds up to a large sum.

☞ When those who called evil good and good evil multiplied, the world's woes were multiplied.

☞ He who is temperamental forgets his learning and becomes steadily foolish.

☞ Some, if a fly falls into their cup, will refuse to drink. Some, if a fly falls into their cup, will throw away the fly and drink. And others, if a fly falls into their soup, will squash the fly and eat the soup. — As there are differing attitudes regarding food, so there are differing attitudes regarding one's mate.

☞ Once a man is deviant and repeats his deviance, it appears to him as permissible.

☞ That which has been transmitted in writing should not be transmitted through speech; that which has been transmitted orally should not be committed to writing.

☞ Personal disgrace is worse than bodily pain.

☞ Anyone who eats in the market place is comparable to a dog.

☞ A temperamental man gains nothing except the ill effects of his temper.

☞ The maximum number of students that can adequately be taught by one teacher is 25. A class of 50 should be split amongst two teachers. If there are 40, we should supply the teacher with an assistant.

☞ A son's actions reflect on his father, but a father's actions do not reflect on his son.

☞ The laws of interest are strict. If one has never greeted his fellow, and, because he has borrowed from him, now greets him, this is forbidden interest.

☞ Man does not banter in the hour of his death.

☞ The body is strong, but fright breaks it. Fright is strong, but wine numbs its potency. Wine is strong, but sleep overcomes it.

☞ A judge should render decisions based only on what his eyes see.

☞ If others have done you much harm, let it appear to you as trivial. If you have done others little harm, let it appear to you as much.

☞ If you possess all virtues but lack humility, you are incomplete, for people will say, "So-and-so would be a great man were it not for his pride."

☞ If you have friends, some of whom criticize you whilst others praise you, love those who criticize you and dislike those who praise you.

☞ In the way man wishes to travel, so is he led along.

☞ Where there is true justice, there is no harmony; where there is harmony, there is no real justice. How can justice be combined with harmony? — In arbitration.

☞ Cry for one who does not know his fate; laugh for one who does not know his fate. Woe to him who cannot tell the difference between good and bad.

☞ It would be surprising if there is anyone in this generation who accepts criticism. For if one is told, "Remove the mote from between your eyes," he would retort, "Remove the beam from between your eyes."

☞ If God abhors idolatry, why does he not abolish it? — If it were something the world did not need, He would abolish it. But consider; idolaters worship the sun, the moon, the stars, and the planets. Should the world be destroyed because of the fools?

☞ The era is determined by its leader. The leader is determined by his era.

☞ A scholar of questionable ancestry takes precedence over an ignorant High Priest.

☞ Man should always eat and drink less than his means, clothe himself according to his means, and honor his wife and children more than his means allow.

☞ He who can prevent wrongdoing in his household but refrains from so doing will be blamed for his household; amongst the inhabitants of his city, he will be blamed for the people in his city; in the whole world, he will be blamed for the wrongdoings of the world.

☞ Man should be accustomed to say, "All that God has done is for ultimate good."

☞ Scholars, the older they grow, the more wisdom they acquire; but the ignorant, the older they grow, the more foolish they become.

☞ Childhood is a crown of roses, old-age a crown of willow rods.

☞ Of all the things God created in this world, He did not create a single thing without purpose.

☞ A prosecutor cannot become a defense attorney.

☞ Do not succumb to anger and you will not transgress; do not drink excessively and you will not transgress.

☞ The sadness caused by a bad dream is sufficient for it and the joy which a good dream brings is sufficient for it.

☞ High office shortens man's days.

☞ He who is arrogant, if a sage, his wisdom slips away from him.

☞ At the gate of the store, there are many brothers and friends; at the gate of poverty, there are neither brothers nor friends.

☞ A dream which is left uninterpreted is like a letter which is not read.

☞ He who runs after greatness, greatness eludes him; but he who runs from greatness, greatness seeks him out.

☞ Prevarication is frequent, truth rare.

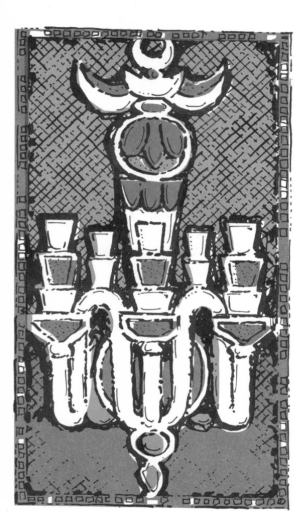

☞ Four types are intolerable; an arrogant poor man, a deceitful rich man, a licentious old man, and one who sets himself over the community irresponsibly.

☞ Happy is the era in which the greater give ear to the smaller.

☞ If a person should tell you, "I have striven but have not found," do not believe him. If he says, "I have not striven but have nevertheless found," do not believe him. If he says, "I have striven and found," believe him.

☞ A flute is musical to nobles, but even if you offer to give it to a commoner, he will refuse it.

☞ He who refrains from retaliation, his own offenses will be overlooked.

☞ Food brings with it the desire to sleep.

☞ A person's voice is not heard by day the way it is heard at night.

☞ He who shares the community's anguish will merit experiencing the community's redemption.

☞ Just as fire is not ignited of its own accord, so too does Torah not endure with him who studies alone.

☞ He who is happy in spite of the suffering that afflicts him brings salvation to the world.

☞ Your own offspring sometimes teaches you reason.

☞ A person should not cause conversation at a meal, lest some food meets the windpipe before the foodpipe and brings another fellow into danger.

☞ One should at all times maintain a pleasant disposition with people.

☞ Man should not raise a bad dog in his house, nor should he install a shaky ladder in his house.

☞ Do not sit too long, as sitting causes piles; do not stand too much, as standing is strenuous for the heart; do not walk too much as walking is harmful to the eyes. Rather spend one-third of your activity in sitting, one-third in standing, and one-third in walking.

☞ Any man who lives without a wife lives without joy, without blessing, and without goodness.

☞ Why are fingers pointed like pegs? — So that if man hears an improper thing he should put the fingers in his ears.

☞ If a man is indigent but refuses to be maintained by welfare, sustenance is offered to him as a gift, and, failing that, as a loan.

☞ Man is allowed to distort the truth in the interests of peace.

☞ Any judge who is a habitual borrower is disqualified from acting as judge.

☞ What is an example of a pious fool? — He who sees a woman drowning in the river and says, "It is not proper for me to gaze upon her and save her."

☞ Righteous people say little, but do much. Say little, but do much.

☞ Man should judge neither one whom he loves nor one whom he hates. For man cannot discern the guilt of one whom he loves nor the innocence of one whom he hates.

☞ Man does not commit an offense unless the spirit of folly has overcome him.

☞ If a rabbinic leader is loved by his community, it is not because he is superior but because he does not rebuke the community for their spiritual neglect.

☞ Regarding the well of a townspeople, if it is a question of their lives and the lives of strangers, the lives of the townspeople have priority.

☞ If you take hold of too much, you take hold of nothing; if you take hold of a little, you will be able to hold it.

☞ He who marries an unfitting mate is as though he had plowed the entire world and sown it with salt.

☞ Eat a third, drink a third, and leave one-third of your stomach empty, so that if you become angry, your stomach will have room to boil.

☞ He who marries for the sake of financial gain will have deficient children.

☞ If part of a testimony has been discredited, the entire testimony is nullified.

☞ Anyone who withholds his employee's wages is as though he had taken his life from him.

☞ One should not remove stones from his domain by throwing them into the public thoroughfare.

☞ Such is the punishment of a liar, that even when he tells the truth, he is not believed.

☞ Children should not be transported for their education from one city to another.

☞ Regarding succession, the son has preference; regarding maintenance, the daughter has preference.

☞ When love is strong, a bed thin as the edge of a blade is sufficient; when love grows weak, the largest bed is not big enough.

☞ Always judge your fellow with a leaning to the side of merit.

☞ The case involving pittance should be as important to you as the case involving thousands.

☞ Be wary of anyone who advises you according to his own nature.

☞ A very tall man should not marry a very tall woman, lest their children be excessively lanky; an abnormally short man should not marry an abnormally short woman lest their children be dwarfs.

☞ Who is mighty? — He who makes of an enemy his friend.

☞ He who has bothered to prepare before the Sabbath will eat on the Sabbath; he who has not prepared before Sabbath, from where shall he eat on the Sabbath?

☞ If one takes payment for judging, his judgments are null and void.

If one takes payment to testify, his testimony is null and void.

☞ What should a man do to live? — He should mortify himself.

What should a man do to die? — He should overindulge in life.

☞ The more property, the more worry.

☞ Go down from your place two or three rungs and sit. It is better to be told "Go up" than to be told "Go down."

☞ It is not incumbent upon you to complete the task, yet you are not free to desist from it.

☞ Which is the correct course for man to pursue? — That which does credit to the one who adopts it and brings him honor from mankind.

☞ In a time when scholars withhold knowledge, disseminate it; when they disseminate knowledge, withhold it.

☞ Any decree which the majority of the population does not accept is null and void.

☞ One should always strive to live in a city just recently populated.

☞ A child does not learn to call "father" and "mother" until he has tasted bread.

☞ If the man emits seed first, the offspring will be a girl; if the woman emits first, the offspring will be a boy.

☞ Even if you hang the heart of a palm tree on a pig, it will still do its thing.

☞ He who is in a position to intercede on behalf of his fellow, but does not, is considered a sinner.

☞ Only a fraction of the praise due a person should be given in his presence, and all the praise due to him in his absence.

☞ If one thinks of performing a good deed but is forcibly prevented from doing it, it is still considered as if he had done it.

☞ The things man does in his youth weaken him in his later years.

☞ Woman entices with her heart and man with his mouth, and this is a superior trait in woman.

☞ Arise early to eat, in the summer because of the heat, and in the winter because of the cold.

☞ Flay carcasses in the street for your wages rather than say "I am a priest or great man and it is below my dignity."

☞ Whoever slanders, whoever accepts slander, and whoever testifies falsely against his fellow deserve to be thrown to the dogs.

☞ He who says he will transgress and repent, will be denied the opportunity to repent.

☞ Wine and pleasant spices inspire the intellect.

☞ One should not promise a child something and then not give it, as he thus teaches the child to lie.

☞ The talk of the child in public is that of his father and mother.

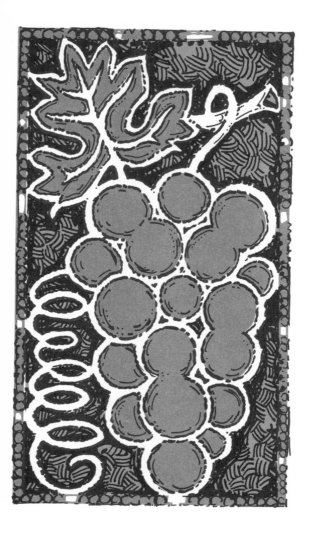

☞ Three types lead a miserable existence; he who is dependent on his neighbor's table, he who is domineered by his wife, and he whose body is ruled by suffering.

☞ He who raises an orphan in his house is considered as having brought the child into the world.

☞ The greater the man, the greater his instinctual energy.

☞ If a man is anxiety-ridden with a problem, he should share it with others.

☞ Two voices cannot be perceived in one ear.

☞ He who repeats anything in another's name should act as if the author of the quote is confronting him.

☞ If you see a student for whom study is as hard as iron, it is because his teacher fails to encourage him.

☞ When a man journeys on the road, he should not eat more than one eats in years of famine.

☞ A woman's weapons are upon her.

☞ If a man marries in his youth, he should marry again in his later years.

☞ Cry for the mourners, not the deceased. He has found his rest, they are left distressed.

☞ It is better to live in companionship than in widowhood.

☞ Prosperity resides only in things over which the eye has no dominion.

☞ It is not the place that honors the man, rather the man who honors the place.

☞ There are three whose lives are lacking; the over-compassionate, the hot-tempered, and the too-squeamish.

47

☞ Who is considered an imbecile? — He who destroys all that is given to him.

☞ Some are industrious and gain, others are industrious and lose; some are lazy and gain, others are lazy and lose.

☞ Do not become dependent on drugs and do not jump in great strides.

☞ Quietude is good for the wise; how much more so for fools.

☞ He who is prone to anger, if a sage, his wisdom slips away from him.

☞ Man should always converse in a dignified language.

☞ We should not rely on miracles.

☞ Do not enter your house suddenly; all the more so your fellow's house.

☞ More than the calf desires to be nursed, the cow desires to nurse.

☞ Better to deal in carcasses than to deal in words.

☞ Once an error has infiltrated, it remains.

☞ A judge should always imagine that a sword lies between his thighs and hell is open beneath him.

☞ Not having seen is not considered proof.

☞ If one decides to be charitable in profusion, he should not diffuse more than one-fifth of his assets, lest he too become dependent on his fellow man.

☞ Ewe follows ewe. Like the acts of the mother, so are the acts of the daughter.

☞ A woman prefers one measure with frivolity to ten measures and abstinence.

☞ A virtuous wife, happy is her husband; the days of his life are doubled.

☞ Man should first build a house and plant a vineyard, and only subsequent to that marry.

☞ A father's loving concern is for his children; the children's loving concern is for their future children.

☞ A man does not act haughtily when confronted by his creditor.

☞ Better is he who affectionately gleams his teeth to his fellow than he who feeds him milk.

☞ No one is poor except him who lacks sense.

☞ Do things for their own sake.

☞ Man should sing his praise in a low voice, and his self-reproach in a loud voice.

☞ A person should not drink from one cup with his eye staring at another.

50

☞ Love your neighbor as yourself — even in demise, choose for him an easy death.

☞ Man is paired with the woman he deserves.

☞ Whoever is faithless, his wife reciprocates his faithlessness.

☞ In the manner which man measures others, so is he measured.

☞ If you are told your friend has died, believe it; if you are told he has become wealthy, do not believe it.

☞ Three things diminish man's strength; anxiety, travel, and transgression.

☞ Amongst mortals, the haughty usually notice the haughty, but the haughty do not notice the modest.

☞ A person should never instill excessive fear in his household.

☞ Anger in a household is like a worm in the sesame plant. Immorality in a household is like a worm in the sesame plant.

☞ Even a poor man who is sustained through charity should himself give to charity.

☞ It is not the mouse that is the thief, rather the hole.

☞ A person who is possessed by haughtiness will eventually be lowered in rank.

☞ If the father does not teach his son a profession it is as though he had taught him thievery.

☞ Even he who is wicked his entire life but repents at the end is not reminded of his wickedness.

☞ It is better for man to commit an offense in private rather than to publicly profane Heaven's name.

☞ He who grants a loan without witnesses puts a stumbling block in front of the blind.

☞ He who regularly declares others unfit reflects on his own defects.

☞ Honor your wife, that your life may be enriched.

☞ Contentiousness prevails in a household only through problems relating to adequate income.

☞ When we are young we are treated as adults; when we are older, we are treated as babies.

☞ A well from which you once drank water, do not throw lumps of earth into it.

☞ One should always belong to the persecuted rather than to the persecutors.

☞ To plea "I do not know" when you should know is considered negligence.

☞ Man is always culpable for his actions, whether unwitting or willful, whether done in a conscious state or in sleep.

☞ Do not criticize your fellow for a fault he shares with you.

☞ Man does not usually commit an offense unless he stands to gain from it.

☞ Happy is he who is employed in perfumes; woe to him who is employed in a tannery.

☞ One's money should always be available for use.

☞ He who forces time is forced back by time, but he who yields to time finds time standing at his side.

☞ If your wife is short, bend down and listen to her.

☞ If a fellow calls you an ass, put a saddle on your back.

☞ It is preferable for man to thrust himself into a fiery furnace rather than publicly shame his neighbor.

☞ Anyone whose mind is not at ease should not pray.

☞ The highest praise is silence. Even a pearl of infinite value, any praise given it detracts from it.

☞ Just as there cannot be wheat without straw, so there cannot be a dream without a measure of nonsense.

☞ Moonlight was created only for the sake of study.

☞ The lender is greater than he who performs charity; but he who forms a partnership with the poor is greater than all.

☞ It is irrelevant whether a man accomplishes much or little, as long as the heart is directed purely towards Heaven.

☞ Three things expand man's spirits: a beautiful dwelling, a beautiful wife, and beautiful clothes.

☞ It is forbidden for man to eat before he feeds his animals.

☞ A bad child in one's house is more unbearable than the most destructive war.

☞ He who is born in the constellation Mars will be a shedder of blood; either a surgeon, a thief, or a slaughterer.

☞ Man is shown in his dreams only what derives from his own thoughts.

☞ Logic is not to be found in the elderly, nor wise counsel in children.

☞ Man is a conglomerate of three partners: God, his father, and his mother.

☞ A man should always pray for personal tranquility even until the last clod of earth covers him.

☞ One is not allowed to take unto himself an animal or bird unless he has prepared adequate sustenance for it.

☞ Verbal wrong is worse than monetary wrong. The former affects the victim's person, the latter only his money.

☞ Man is related to himself; therefore no person can testify to his own wickedness.

☞ Man is obliged to bless God in bad times in the same manner that he blesses God in good times.

☞ Any man who has no wife is not a true man.

☞ First adorn yourself before demanding that others adorn themselves.

☞ Anyone who publicly shames his fellow is as though he had shed blood.

☞ As the sun rises illness lightens.

☞ He who causes his fellow to perform a good deed is considered as if he himself had done it.

☞ He who lends on interest denies the fundamental faith of Judaism.

☞ Before man eats and drinks he has two hearts; after he eats and drinks, he has only one heart.

☞ Woe to him who has no courtyard yet makes a gate for it.

☞ A fool teaches his child nonsense.

☞ We do not cancel a child's studies even in order to build the Temple.

☞ Teach your tongue to say "I do not know," lest you err and stumble through your error.

☞ The diligent student will learn of his own accord. If a student is indolent, place him next to the diligent one.

☞ Which is the upright path for man to choose? — Let him love criticism, for as long as there is constructive criticism, contentment, good, and blessing come to the world, and evil leaves the world.

Which is the upright path for man to choose?— Let him be scrupulously honest.

☞ Love has no concern for rules of protocol.

Hate has no regard for rules of protocol.

☞ What should a man do to become enriched? — He should make much business and handle it honestly.

☞ He who causes others to do good is greater than the doer.

☞ One should never relate his fellow's good qualities, for by so doing he brings about discussion of his bad qualities.

☞ He who suspects his fellow of a fault which he has not, must ask his forgiveness.

61

☞ Conflict is like an opening made by a stream of water that expands as the water gushes through.

☞ Man should at all times associate with good people.

☞ The world maintains its stability only because of those who restrain themselves in times of conflict.

☞ Keep your distance from things hideous and what appears hideous.

☞ Man should not be joyous amongst the weeping, nor should he weep amongst the joyous. He should not be awake amongst the sleeping, nor should he sleep amongst those who are awake.

☞ If you have done much good, let it seem to you as little. Say, "Not from my own have I done good, rather from what has been granted me."

☞ The glory of wisdom is in humility.